You Are F✿cking Beautiful

SWEARY AFFIRMATIONS AND FUNNY QUOTES FOR BADASS WOMEN

SASSY QUOTES PRESS

Hello Beautiful

You are a ray of fucking sunshine. Of course, even an awesome ray like yourself has to deal with shade from assholes and bullshit.

That's why this book exists: to brighten the fuck out of your day with sparkly humor and badass positivity.

You know that laughter and positive thinking are healthy and that swearing feels good. Now, even scientists agree that profanity is healthy. Swearing reduces stress, anxiety, and physical pain and boosts strength.*

That's right. *Swearing is self care, bitch.*

So get ready for a megadose of sweary humor and positivity to spark joy and laughter in your day. In this book, you'll find:

- Powerful affirmations for loving the fuck out of yourself
- Badass motivational quotes to fire you up
- 25 Creative Ways to Say "Fuck Off" when dealing with assholes
- Page after page of delightfully irreverent humor that cuts through the bullshit and keeps you laughing

*Not doing fucking citations, but you can google "swearing is good for you" if you're curious. Or ask a robot. Those motherfuckers are everywhere these days. *Make AI your bitch.*

Whether you need a friendly reminder of how fucking awesome you are, or just want to laugh and relax, this book is here for you. Morning, noon, and night.

Oh, and so are the **100 bonus affirmation cards**! You can print out your favorite quotes and put them where you'll see them daily. Perfect for journals, vision boards, or sharing with your badass friends and family. (The instant access download link is at the back of this book.)

So let's fucking go, sunshine!

You are an
amazing human.

You have an
awesome ability
to learn and grow.

You will always
be worthy of love.

Thanks for coming
to my Ted talk, bitch

You are a
fucking delight

What's your
beauty secret?
Drink water
and glow like
fucking sunshine?

You always
spark joy, bitch

You fucking rock.
Please don't worry
about assholes.
I'll take care of them.
xoxo Karma

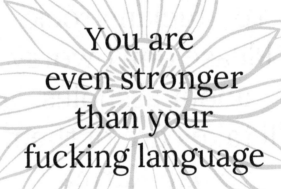

You are
even stronger
than your
fucking language

You are a fucking star.
But keep reaching for
the stars anyway.
Because you're
not a lazy star.
#Fuckingstargoals

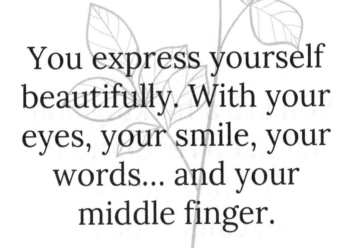

You express yourself beautifully. With your eyes, your smile, your words... and your middle finger.

Take a deep breath,
check your nails,
and make shit happen

Invest in yourself.
Think of it as
Bitchcoin

Your opinions,
like your heart,
are fucking gold.

Hello, badass.
Will you be operating
in light mode or
dark mode today?

You did not
wake up today to
follow assholes

You float over
fuckery like a
badass butterfly

You are smart, funny,
kind and talented.
And the best part
is that you can have
a friendly chat
with yourself any
time you want,
you lucky bitch.

You attract
and radiate
badass energy

Swearing *is*
your love language

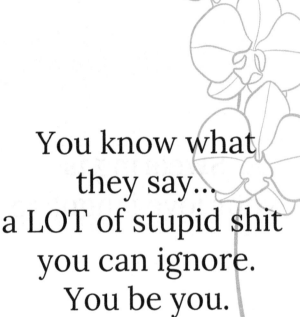

You know what
they say...
a LOT of stupid shit
you can ignore.
You be you.

Think big.
Start small.
Keep fucking going.

Remember your *Why*
so you can power
through your
What the Fucks?!

Honest question.
Do you ever
get tired of being so
fucking awesome?

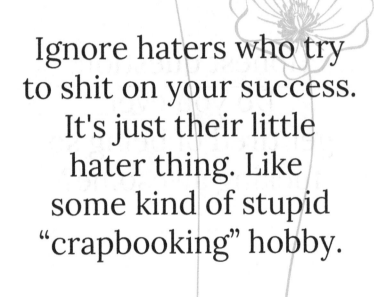

Ignore haters who try
to shit on your success.
It's just their little
hater thing. Like
some kind of stupid
"crapbooking" hobby.

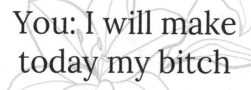

You: I will make
today my bitch

Today: As you wish,
Your Hotness

You're probably
the kind of badass
who knows how to
fold a fitted sheet. Now,
that's some badass shit.

When your brilliance
throws a glare on
your screen
#Awesomebitchproblems

You are a fucking gem.
Haters will try, but
nothing can dim
your shine.

Forgive assholes.
They hate that.

Kill them with kindness...
Or torture them
with sarcasm.
You have options.

Forgive the sports
analogy, but grab
today by the balls

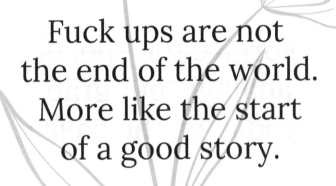

Fuck ups are not
the end of the world.
More like the start
of a good story.

You are fucking magical.
We're talking sparkly
unicorn leaping over
rainbows with kittens
on your back kind
of energy.

You are fucking
beautiful...
inside and out

Say "Sayonara" to
imposter syndrome,
that toxic bitch

Everything you need
to succeed is within you.
You're like a beautiful,
walking, talking purse
filled with useful shit.

There's a word for
women like you:

Ambitchious
You have the attitude
to reach higher
altitude.

Assholes are no match
for your smokey eye,
side eye combo.

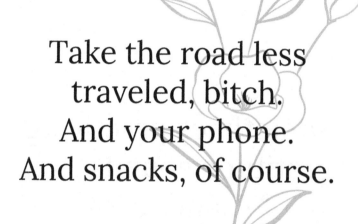

Take the road less
traveled, bitch.
And your phone.
And snacks, of course.

Sometimes practicing gratitude sounds like, "Thanks a lot motherfucker."

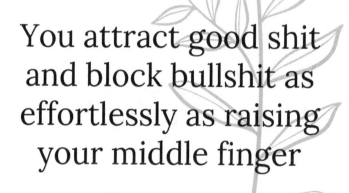

You attract good shit
and block bullshit as
effortlessly as raising
your middle finger

You're too grounded
to give a flying fuck

If swear words are
"colorful language,"
maybe add
"Fucking Artist"
to your profiles?

Happy Fucking New Day
Just pointing out that
you can try new things
any time you want, not
just in January

Better than yesterday
is a worthy fucking goal

If you wouldn't say it
to a friend, don't say it
to yourself, bitch.
xoxo Your Sweary
Godmother

Be bold.
Be brave.
Be your badass self.

Anything is possible
with a little sunshine
and swearing

May your bucket list
be as long as your
fuck-it list

Mean people are not happy people. But it's still hard to be sad for those assholes.

Some days you
just have to drop
a few f-bombs and
blow some shit up

Do your best
and fuck the rest

Be kind.
Unless someone
is being an asshole.
Then, be kind of bitchy.

Today's plan:
clear boundaries,
grateful heart, strong
fucking language

It's a beautiful day
to get shit done

Did you know that the average person says 80 swear words a day. Fuckin' amateurs.

You could teach a
badass masterclass

Don't worry what assholes think. Thinking is not one of their strengths.

"Fuck it" is the
"aloha" of swearing.
It can mean
"Fuck no,"
"Fuck yes,"
or whatever the fuck
you want it to mean.

Take a deep breath
and imagine that
another badass bitch
is giving thanks for you.
Because they are.

Tell negative thoughts
to go to Hell

You do amazing things
every fucking day.
And some days, just
getting out of bed will
feel like an amazing
accomplishment.
Every win counts, bitch.

Your inner critic
is a total bitch.
Ignore her.

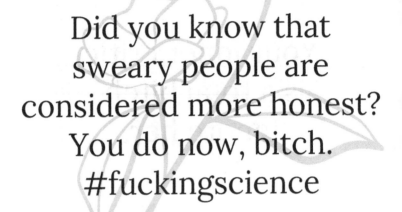

Did you know that
sweary people are
considered more honest?
You do now, bitch.
#fuckingscience

Look on the fucking
bright side

You are a
fucking force
of nature

What goals do you want
to crush with your
awesomeness?
You are
un-fucking-stoppable

Do epic shit.
And, yes,
epic naps count.

Failure is the only "F" word that should be censored. It just means discovering ways that don't work. That's valuable fucking knowledge.

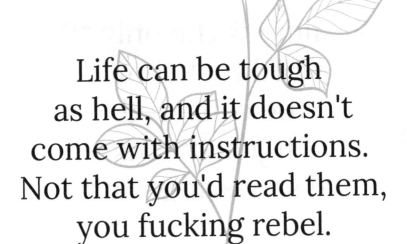

Life can be tough
as hell, and it doesn't
come with instructions.
Not that you'd read them,
you fucking rebel.

Don't trip over shit
that's behind you

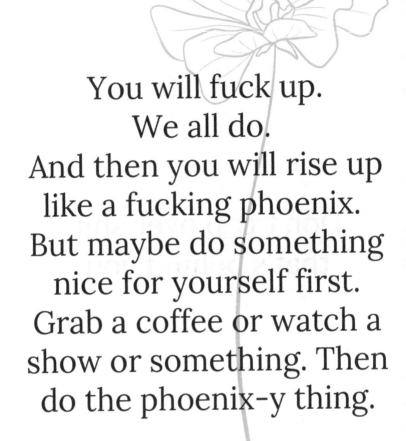

You will fuck up.
We all do.
And then you will rise up
like a fucking phoenix.
But maybe do something
nice for yourself first.
Grab a coffee or watch a
show or something. Then
do the phoenix-y thing.

Damn, you're good

You don't swear
at the top of your lungs.
You perform.

Make yourself a
fucking priority

Self care
is the best
middle finger
you can ever give

Love the fuck
out of yourself

Don't let a shitty day
trick you into
thinking you have
a shitty life

Cringe attack
survival tip:
Let that shit go

You are worthy as fuck.

Your grateful heart
is a magnet for
more great shit

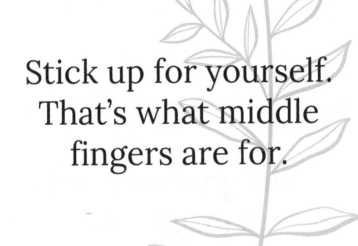

Stick up for yourself.
That's what middle
fingers are for.

Keep saving your
fucks, and before
you know it, you'll
have enough to live in
everyone-fuckoff-town

It's always fuck this shit
o'clock somewhere

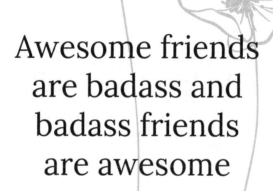

Awesome friends
are badass and
badass friends
are awesome

Be kind as fuck
to yourself

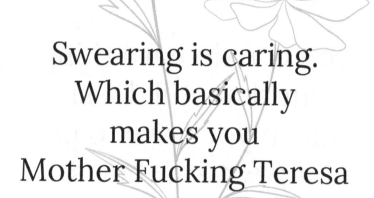

Swearing is caring.
Which basically
makes you
Mother Fucking Teresa

You can do hard things.
But that still doesn't
mean you have to put
up with assholes.

"You fucking rock"
is a fucking
understatement

Boss bitch is a
good look for you

You don't owe haters the
time of day, much less
your precious fucks.

Recharge your soul.
Do more of what makes
you fucking happy.

Don't compare your
real life to someone
else's fake as fuck
highlight reel

You are bullshit proof

"Fuck no"
is a perfectly
acceptable way
to communicate
boundaries.

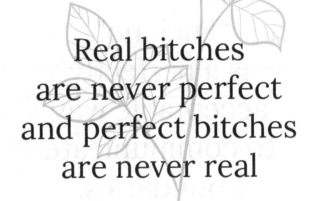

Real bitches
are never perfect
and perfect bitches
are never real

Are you tired of hearing
"You are enough"?
Tough titties.
Because you are.
Abso-fucking-lutely.

Today's forecast:
100% chance of bullshit.
0% chance of you
giving a fuck.

Looks aren't everything,
bitch. But at least
you have them
if you need them.

Bloom where
you're planted, bitch

You can't swear
all the time.
You need sleep, too.

Fuckity fuck fuck.
Mean people suck.

25 Creative Ways to Say "Fuck Off"

Assholes don't deserve your precious fucks. So, here's a handy list of insults so you can clap back and keep going.

1. Nice. You've got that asshole-hair-don't-care vibe going on.
2. You'd be great on that new show... The Great American Fuck Off.
3. Do you use regular toilet paper? Or do you have to buy special bullshit wipes for your mouth?
4. I wouldn't call you a huge asshole. I prefer anally gifted.
5. You spark sadness. And nobody wants a used asshole, so kindly Kondo yourself into the trash.
6. Fuck-ups aren't like push-ups. Your goal shouldn't be doing as many as you can.
7. Damn it. I put my phone on Do Not Disturb, but you're still here.
8. You're proof that AI isn't a big deal. You've been faking intelligence your whole life.
9. Let me guess. You grew up in Whatthefuckville.
10. You're not a total asshole. You're at least 30% shithead.
11. You can't act like an asshole and think people will still like you. You're not a cat.
12. If it walks like a dick and talks like a dick, it's probably a you.
13. I've got a great deal for you. Get 10 fuck offs the asshole special just for shutting up.
14. A dumbass like you could only have graduated from Fuck U.

15. Good news. Size does matter and you are an enormous dick.
16. Living with intention is good. But why did you intend to be an asshole?
17. Seeing you reminds me... I need to get more "Bitch-B-Gone."
18. You look like a million I-don't-give-a-fucks.
19. I just want you to be happy. And the key to happiness is getting the fuck away from me.
20. Your face is truly epic. We're talking "launch a thousand shits" epic.
21. Your hormones must be out of whack. If you want them whacked back into place, I'd love to help.
22. Giving 110% is great. But not when it comes to being an asshole.
23. This is an asshole-free zone. I'm going to have to ask you to back up. Preferably down a flight of stairs.
24. Tourists must love taking pictures with you. "Look at me, standing next to the World's Biggest Asshole!"
25. No offense, butt. That's it. That's the insult.

Bonus Gift

Thank you for choosing

For *instant access* to your printable companion set of ·100 *Sweary Affirmation Cards,* please visit

www.sassyquotespress.com/yafb

No email signup required

You will receive a high-quality PDF file that includes 100 cards and printing instructions.

These beautiful floral designs are perfect for vision boards, journals and planners. You can post them on your mirror, walls or anywhere you'll see them daily. Or share them with your badass friends!

Questions? Comments? I would love to hear from you! Please email me at jen@sassyquotespress.com

More Fun From
Sassy Quotes Press

Check out our hilarious planners, coloring books
and gratitude journals with lots of sweary quotes inside.

Visit
amazon.com/author/
sassyquotespress

Or scan this QR code
with your device

A favor please 🩶

Would you take a quick minute to leave this book a **rating/review on Amazon**?

It makes a HUGE difference, and I would really appreciate it!

Thank you!
Jen@SassyQuotesPress.com

IMPORTANT: If the book you received was not printed correctly or was damaged during shipping, *please return to Amazon for a perfectly printed copy or a refund*. I hate when that happens! Amazon does a great job printing and shipping books, but errors do happen occasionally. Thank you for understanding!